PENGUIN

by **CAROLINE ARNOLD**

Photographs by
RICHARD HEWETT

Morrow Junior Books · New York

Library of Congress Cataloging-in-Publication Data. Arnold, Caroline. Penguin. Summary: discusses the physical characteristics, habits, and life cycle of the Magellanic penguin, a native of South America. Focuses on the lives of Humberto and Domino, a pair of Magellanics at the San Francisco Zoo, as they prepare a nest and care for their baby chick, Uno. 1. Magellanic penguin—Juvenile literature. 2. Penguins—Juvenile literature. [1. Magellanic penguin. 2. Penguins] I. Hewett, Richard, ill. II. Title. QL696.S473A76 1988 598.4'41 87-31458 ISBN 0-688-07706-4 ISBN 0-688-07707-2 (lib. bdg.)

ACKNOWLEDGMENTS

We are extremely grateful to the San Francisco Zoo for their cooperation on this project, and we thank all the zoo staff and volunteers who helped us to learn about penguins and to photograph them. In particular, we want to thank Nancy Schofield, Curator of Birds (pictured above); penguin keepers Elisabeth Ryan and Scott Bentall; Gail Hedberg, animal health technician; Suzanne Dempsay and Irene Donovan, avian hand-rearing technicians; and Ellen Newman, Director of Public Relations. And, as always, we appreciate the enthusiastic support of our editor, Andrea Curley.

POKING her head out of nest hole number sixteen, the female penguin watched her mate approach. Waddling on short, sturdy legs, he was bringing her a piece of pampas grass to add to their nest.

Like many of the other penguin pairs on their island, they will soon have two eggs in their nest. When the eggs hatch, they will have hungry baby penguins to feed.

These birds are among fifty-two Magellanic penguins that inhabit the newly remodeled penguin exhibit at the San Francisco Zoo in California. Originally from an island off the coast of Chile, the penguins came to the zoo in 1984.

When they arrived, each bird was given a numbered band that was fastened around its wing. The bands helped the zoo staff to identify each penguin so they could monitor its health and activities. Soon the keepers learned to recognize each bird and, in some cases, they gave the penguins their own names as well. The two birds occupying nest hole number sixteen had been nicknamed Humberto and Domino.

The penguins seemed to like their new home at the zoo. The island and the pool around it were designed to be as much like the penguins' native South American habitat as possible. It was landscaped with black volcanic rocks similar to those at the penguins' home in Chile, and it was planted with grasses and shrubs that could be used for nesting material. Every other day the penguin keepers cleaned the island and filled the pool with fresh water.

The penguin exhibit, named Tuxedo Junction, is one of the most popular at the zoo. Everybody seems to love the comical creatures that look more like plump little gentlemen in formal dress than birds. The colony, which is the largest in captivity, is also part of a large research program that allows scientists to study these amazing animals and learn more about them.

Most people think of penguins as birds of ice and snow. However, only two species, the Adelie and emperor penguins, are native to the Antarctic. The rest live in warmer climates, some as far north as the Equator. All penguins live in the Southern Hemisphere. They are found along the coasts of South America, Africa, Australia, and New Zealand. Although cartoons sometimes show them with Eskimos and polar bears, penguins have never been at the North Pole. All penguins spend most of their lives in the water, coming to shore chiefly during the breeding season.

The seventeen species of penguins are divided into six groups. Members of one group, which includes the Adelies, gentoos, and chinstraps, have long, brushlike tails. The two largest penguins, the emperor and the king, form another group. The emperor penguin, which stands 3½ feet (1 meter) tall and weighs up to 90 pounds (41 kilograms), is the largest of all penguins. The smallest penguin is the little blue, which is only 16 inches (.4 meter) tall and weighs less than 2½ pounds (1 kilogram.) The little blue, sometimes called the fairy penguin, and the yellow-eyed penguin each form a group. The six species of crested penguins, which wear tufts of long yellow feathers on each side of their heads, form one as well.

A king penguin, one of the largest species, looks down at two little blue penguins, the smallest of all penguins.

The last group of penguins includes the four species of warm-weather penguins—the Magellanic, Humboldt (sometimes called the Peruvian), black-footed, and Galapagos penguins. Although found in different locations in the wild, the appearance and behavior of these four species are similar. The scientific name of these penguins is *Spheniscus*, with the Magellanics being called *Spheniscus magellanicus*. In Latin, *spheniscus* means "wedge-shaped" and refers to the penguins' powerful, wedge-shaped wings. Most zoo penguins are members of the *Spheniscus* group because they adapt easily to temperate climates.

All of the *Spheniscus* penguins make a distinctive braying sound much like that of a donkey. For that reason, the black-footed penguins are sometimes called jackass penguins. To make this sound, a penguin puffs up its chest, stretches its neck, and emits a series of bark-like honks. Penguins bray to call to each other and to attract mates. Sometimes two penguins bray together in a kind of duet. In a large colony, the noise created by thousands of braying penguins is enormous.

The Magellanic penguins are named after the Portuguese explorer Ferdinand Magellan, who was the first European to record sighting this unusual family of birds. Magellan explored the coasts of South America and discovered what is now called the Strait of Magellan on his historic trip around the world between 1519 and 1522.

In the wild, Magellanic penguins are found in the Strait of Magellan and the coastal regions of Argentina, Chile, and the Falkland Islands. Like all penguin species, they like to nest in large colonies called rookeries. One of the most famous is at Punta Tombo, in Argentina, where there are over a million birds. There are more Magellanic penguins in the world than any other kind.

An adult Magellanic penguin is just over 2 feet (.6 meter) tall and weighs about 7 pounds (3.2 kilograms). All birds have black backs, white undersides, and distinctive white rings around the face and belly. Although a male is usually slightly heavier and has a larger, more massive head and broader bill, it is extremely difficult to tell males and females apart. It was only after the birds paired off during the first mating season that the zoo staff could tell which were males and which were females.

Once mated, a penguin pair stays together for the rest of their lives.

A pair of penguins may nest for as many as twenty successive seasons, usually returning to the same nest hole each year. This was Humberto and Domino's third nesting season at the zoo.

In the Southern Hemisphere penguins usually begin nesting in September. However, in Northern Hemisphere zoos, where the seasons are reversed, they begin to nest in March. Wild breeding colonies are usually located on bleak stretches of coastline, sometimes dotted with low bushes. Although some penguins nest under bushes, most prefer to dig a burrow in the ground.

Male penguin (left); female penguin (right).

In the wild, a pair of Magellanic penguins use their feet and bills to dig the burrow hole, which can be as long as 6 feet (1.8 meters). At the end of the burrow is a chamber big enough for both birds to lie down and turn around. There the penguins build a nest by making a small mound of sticks, pebbles, dried leaves, grass, or whatever they can find. The burrow protects the eggs and young birds from the weather as well as from enemies such as gulls and other large birds.

At the zoo, Humberto and Domino did not need to dig a burrow hole because the island already had permanent fiberglass holes. These were covered with dirt and rocks so that they would be much like the penguins' wild nesting sites.

All the nest holes on the island were identified, and careful records were kept of which birds lived in which holes. Each day during the nesting season the zoo staff checked all the nests.

One morning in early April one of the penguin keepers reached into Humberto and Domino's nest. Nestled in the dried pampas grass was a smooth oval egg. It was white, about 3 inches (76 millimeters) long, and pointed at one end. Usually a female penguin lays two eggs in the nest, so the keepers were not surprised to find another egg there four days later. Humberto and Domino took turns incubating the eggs—sitting on them to keep them warm and moist.

Most penguin eggs hatch between thirty-eight and forty-two days after being laid. Each day the penguin keepers counted all the eggs and made a note if any appeared ready to hatch. Often the baby penguin, called a chick, can be heard peeping inside the shell a few days before hatching. If the chick had made a small crack in the shell, called the pip, then the penguin keepers knew that the egg would probably hatch within the next two or three days.

By the second week in May, Humberto and Domino had been sitting on their nest for about five-and-a-half weeks. The zoo keepers knew that their eggs would hatch soon. On the morning of the thirty-ninth day after the first egg was laid, one of the zoo keepers reached into the nest. Underneath Humberto was a tiny, fuzzy chick. Its feathers were still damp, so they knew it must have been just an hour or so old.

The newly hatched chick, which weighed about 3½ ounces (100 grams), was blind and helpless. Its eyes will be closed for the first few days of life, but since it is dark inside the burrow, the chick has no need to see. It can tell its parents where it is with tiny cheeps. Penguin parents learn to recognize the cheeps of their own chicks and can distinguish them from the cheeps of other birds.

The penguin keeper inspected the chick to make sure that it was healthy and alert. Because it was the first egg to hatch, she decided to name the chick Uno, meaning "one" in Spanish. As soon as she was finished, she put Uno back into the nest. There its parents would keep it warm and dry and feed it when it got hungry.

Like all baby birds, young penguin chicks are hungry soon after they are hatched. In the wild, the penguin parents take turns going to the sea to hunt for small fish, squid, or other sea animals that are their food. When the parent returns to the nest, it regurgitates, or coughs up, what it has eaten and feeds its chicks the partly digested food.

At the zoo, the penguins are fed fish two times a day. Each bird is individually fed 2 pounds (.9 kilogram) or more of whole herring. At each feeding it also gets one fish stuffed with pills containing vitamins, minerals, and other nutrients needed by seagoing animals.

At every feeding session a zoo volunteer records exactly how many fish each bird has eaten. In this way the zoo staff can make sure that all the penguins get enough food. A parent bird feeding a growing chick has been known to eat as many as sixteen herrings at a feeding. Sometimes the penguin keepers make notes on their gloves to remind them which birds still need their daily vitamin fish. Disposable sterile gloves are always worn by the keepers to make sure that no diseases are carried between the island and other parts of the zoo.

Like most animals, penguins need to drink water every day. At the zoo they have plenty of fresh water in their pond. However, in the wild, the penguins live in the sea and usually must drink salt water. Special glands in their bodies remove the salt from the water. The salt comes out in liquid form and drips down grooves in the side of the penguin's beak.

A penguin's heavy beak is strong. Because the sharp, pointed tip can inflict a painful wound, the penguin keepers had to be careful when reaching into the nests. The parent birds did not like their chicks being handled and often tried to peck the keepers. Usually the keepers found it easiest to remove the parent birds before checking the nests.

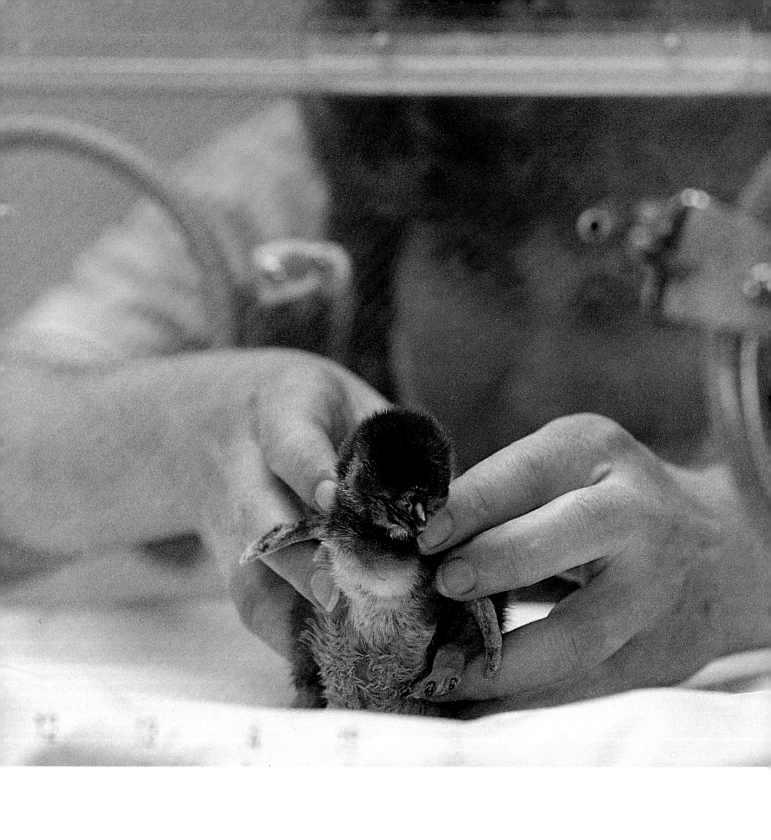

Each day, when the zoo keepers came to the island, they examined all the chicks. They wanted to make sure that the parents were doing a good job of taking care of their young. Most of the time in the wild, penguin parents successfully raise only one of their chicks. At the zoo, each chick is important, and by carefully monitoring the birds, the staff can help all the chicks to survive.

When the second egg in Humberto and Domino's nest hatched, Uno was already four days old. Uno was stronger and ate most of the food at feeding times. Because the younger chick did not seem to be gaining weight fast enough, the zoo keepers decided to take it out of the nest and put it in the zoo hospital. There it would be kept warm in an incubator and fed a special penguin chick formula.

Any chick that appeared to be weak, or was not getting enough food or water, was taken to the zoo hospital. By the end of the nesting season a total of nine chicks were taken out of their nests and brought to the hospital. There, each chick was given a colored wing band for identification. However, like the penguins on the island, each chick had its own personality, and the zoo keepers soon gave them nicknames. They decided to call Humberto and Domino's second chick Squeaker because it always seemed to be cheeping for more food. Squeaker had learned that when the keepers came near it usually meant feeding time.

In the hospital, human "parents" cared for the chicks in much the same way as the penguin parents took care of the eight chicks that remained on the island. A mixture of cream, pureed fish, krill, vitamins, and other nutrients was fed to the chicks through a tube. In the beginning, Squeaker and the other tiny chicks had to be fed seven or eight times a day. As the chicks grew, the staff gradually reduced the number of feedings. By the time the chicks were forty-five days old, they needed to be fed only twice a day. By then they were also being fed whole fish.

Just like the chicks that remained on the island, the chicks in the zoo hospital were weighed once a day. A healthy penguin chick grows rapidly, doubling its weight every few days. By the time a chick is a month old, it weighs more than 4½ pounds (2,000 grams), more than twenty times its weight at hatching.

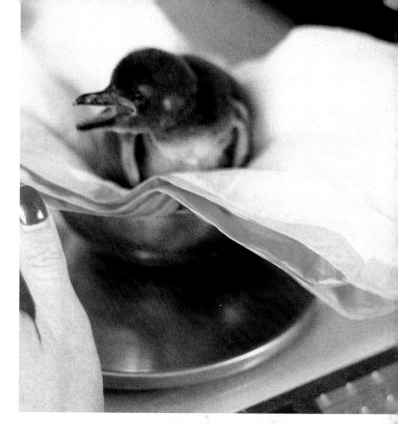

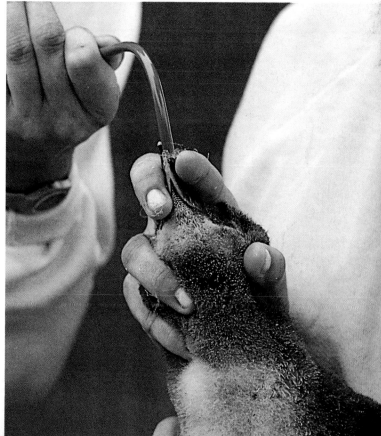

As the chicks in the hospital grew, they no longer needed to stay in the incubator. At the age of two weeks they were moved to a container that was at room temperature. At four weeks the young penguins could stay in an outdoor enclosure most of the time. Although the penguins remained in the hospital area at night and for feeding, during the day they were moved to the Children's Zoo, where zoo visitors could see the birds up close.

Like many animals raised by humans, Squeaker and the young hand-reared penguins became used to being around people very early in life. Many of them remained quite tame even after they became part of the group on the penguin island. At the zoo, as in the wild, the penguins seemed to have little fear of people, and appeared to be curious about the keepers who came to their island.

One morning, when Uno was five weeks old, a penguin keeper came to the nest and took it out. Like the chicks in the hospital, the chicks on the island were checked once a week for overall development. By measuring and comparing features such as weight, height, feather growth, bill development, and wing length, the staff could learn more about the growth of young penguins. This information helped them to keep the penguins healthy and to understand more about how they grow.

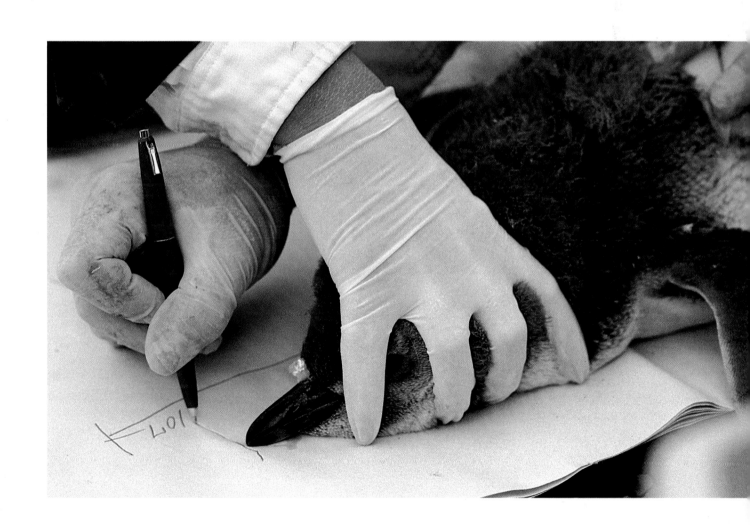

During the first few weeks of its life, Uno had stayed deep in the nest hole. Although it began to peer out of the entrance when it was four weeks old, it was not until six weeks that Uno was ready to venture outside. At first, Uno did not stay out long and waddled back in as soon as it became tired.

Humberto and Domino were extremely protective of their chick and shooed away any adult penguins that came too close to it. Much of their time was spent keeping their chick's feathers smooth and clean.

When Uno became hungry, it leaned toward one of its parents and cheeped as loud as it could. Although the parent seemed to ignore the cheeps at first, after a few minutes it regurgitated food and allowed the chick to eat.

As Uno got older, the zoo keepers coming to the island at feeding time began to give it fish, too. By the time the chick is two months old it will be eating the same diet as the adult penguins, and Humberto and Domino will no longer have to feed it.

During its first few times out of the nest, Uno was cautious, but as it gained confidence, it began to wander away and explore the area around the nest. However, Humberto and Domino were careful to keep their chick away from the water's edge.

When a penguin chick is hatched, it is covered with soft, gray down feathers. These help keep it warm, but they are not waterproof. If a young penguin falls into deep water before its juvenile feathers grow in, it may drown. Uno's juvenile feathers began to appear when it was about five weeks old. They grew in first on the lower part of the body, gradually pushing out the soft down feathers. A chick with partially grown feathers looks as if it is wearing a furry gray cape with a hood. Within eight weeks the mottled brown juvenile feathers are complete. The black-and-white adult feathers do not come in until the penguin's third year.

Unlike the large, lightweight feathers of birds that fly, a penguin has small, tightly packed feathers. They lie close to the body and number more than seventy per square inch. These feathers keep the birds warm and dry.

At the base of its tail a penguin has an oil gland called the preen gland. When preening—cleaning and smoothing its feathers—the penguin dips its bill into the oil and spreads it over its feathers to make them waterproof. Penguins spend much of their time preening and even do it when they are in the water. Pairs of penguins often preen each other.

Once a year penguins lose their old feathers and grow new ones. This is called molting. Molting takes place after the breeding season. While preparing to molt, the penguins often eat three to four times the usual amount of food to build up fat. The fat provides energy necessary for feather growth. Also, since penguins often eat little or no food during the month when molting takes place, their fat provides them with an extra reserve of energy at this time.

Penguins are so well prepared for cold weather that sometimes they get too hot. To cool off, a penguin may fluff up its feathers, as if it were opening a set of blinds, or it may open its mouth and pant. The pink skin on the face and feet of Magellanic penguins allows heat to escape from the blood that flows near the surface of the skin. If necessary, a penguin can also go into its burrow or into the water to get cool.

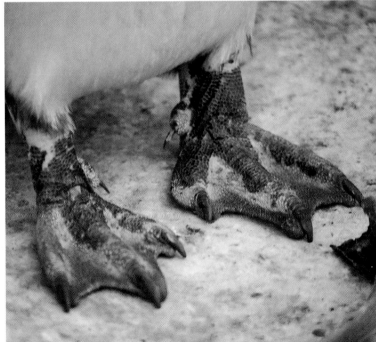

Although Uno did not go into the water at first, it did watch the other birds swim in the pool from the opening of its burrow. A penguin chick usually takes its first swim when it is about seven or eight weeks old. Like all penguins, the Magellanics are excellent swimmers. Plummeting like torpedoes into the pool, they dive, turn, and leap across the water with ease.

In the wild, Magellanics often travel great distances from the nesting grounds after they have finished breeding. Some penguins remain at or near their breeding grounds all year, although others are known to travel up to 1,980 miles (3,153 kilometers) away. Usually they are found swimming in small groups. When swimming long distances, penguins sometimes leap over the water in the same way that dolphins do. To rest, the birds float on their backs, raising their feet like tiny sails. Penguins are completely at home in the water, sometimes spending days there before returning to land. Adult wild Magellanics spend about five months of the year mostly at sea and the rest mainly on shore.

Penguins cannot fly, but they are able to swim faster than any other bird, cruising at about 15 miles (24 kilometers) per hour. Their powerful wings rotate to provide speed, and their tails and feet are used for steering. Penguins rely on speed to escape from their enemies in the ocean.

The penguin's black-and-white coloring, which makes them so visible on land, helps them to hide in the sea. Although the penguins are easy to see in the water of the pool at the zoo, at sea their black backs blend into the darkness of the water. From below, their white undersides are hard to see against the sky.

The main predators of penguins in the sea are leopard seals, sea lions, fur seals, and killer whales. Out of the water they have almost no enemies except for large birds that prey on eggs and young chicks.

No water bird is better adapted to the cold ocean currents where penguins live. Their short wings make excellent paddles when swimming, a layer of fat keeps their plump bodies warm, and their sleek, tightly packed feathers keep them dry.

Unlike birds that fly, whose bones are hollow to make them light-weight, penguins have heavy bones that help them to swim under water. Emperor penguins, the champion divers among penguins, can dive to depths of almost 900 feet (274 meters) and stay under water for almost 20 minutes. However, like all birds, penguins need to breathe air. So even though they can dive to great depths, they must always return to the surface of the water for air.

A young Magellanic penguin is dependent on its parent or human substitute for about eight to nine weeks. When it leaves its parents and becomes independent, we say that it has fledged.

When Uno and the island chicks were able to leave their parents, they were taken to the zoo hospital to join the hand-reared penguins in a large outdoor enclosure. There Uno and Squeaker had a chance to get to know each other and to become used to the zoo feeding routine. When all the juvenile penguins were re-turned to the island about a month later, they were slightly smaller than the adults, duller in color, and without the distinctive rings around the face.

During their first year the young penguins will stick together. Magellanic penguins are not ready to breed until they are at least two years old. As they mature and get their handsome tuxedo markings, the birds will find mates and pair off. Only then will the keepers know for sure which of the young penguins are males and which are females.

Although no one is sure how long penguins can live in the wild, some in zoos have lived more than thirty years. The breeding program at the San Francisco Zoo has been so successful that each year some of the penguins must be sold or traded to other zoos to keep the island from becoming too crowded. Since most people do not have a chance to go to the Southern Hemisphere and see penguins in the wild, as more zoos get penguins it helps more people get to know these fascinating birds.

Penguins are amazingly well-adapted to their natural environment, which to us often appears to be harsh and uninviting. However, as people have altered that environment, some species of penguins have become extinct and others have be-come endangered. In the past, many penguins were killed for food and oil, and their nests were raided for eggs. Today, all penguins are protected by law. Nevertheless, excessive fishing in some areas has endangered penguins by reducing their food supply. Perhaps the greatest danger to the survival of penguins and all sea life is increasing pollution—oil spills and chemical wastes in the ocean.

People have always been intrigued by penguins and have wanted to learn more about them. There is something particularly appealing about birds that walk upright and seem to be dressed like little people. As scientists study penguins, both in zoos and in the wild, we will better learn how to ensure their future.

Index

Photographs are in **boldface.**